MAX
IN AMERICA · No 2

Illustrated by **Oscar Mesa**

Adapted by **Raymond C. Clark**

Interplay ESL • Communicating in the Culture

PRO LINGUA   ASSOCIATES

Published by Pro Lingua Associates
15 Elm Street
Brattleboro, Vermont 05301

802-257-7779

SAN 216-0579

Communicating in the Culture: Max in America is an adaption of the **Poly Training Tape: English,** copyright © 1972 by The Experiment in International Living. Permission to use the illustrations and some of the text from the original is granted by The Experiment Press. The authors on the 1972 Experiment Deutsche Grammophon Gesellschaft project were Alvino Fantini, director, Beatrix Fantini, David P. Rein, Priscilla Martin, and Raymond C. Clark; the illustrator, Oscar Mesa.

The Experiment Press plans to announce the publication of a revised edition of the **Poly Training Tape: English,** self-study materials including tapes and cassettes. For information, write to The Experiment Press, S.I.T., Brattleboro, Vermont 05301 or Pro Lingua Associates.

ISBN 0-86647-025-5

This book was set in Electra by Stevens Graphics of Brattleboro, Vermont, and printed and bound by Murray Printing in Kendallsville, Indiana. Cover by Marle Stevens. Book designed by Arthur A. Burrows.

Printed in the United States of America.

Acknowledgements

This book is an adaptation of a self-study English program of texts and cassettes called *Poly Training Tape: English*. It was produced in 1970 by The Experiment in International Living and Deutsche Grammophon Gesellschaft. The original materials (there was also a similar program for learning Spanish) were not designed for classroom use, but for several years they were adapted for the classroom by a number of English and Spanish teachers at The Experiment in International Living in Brattleboro, Vermont. The success of these teacher-made adaptations is, in part, responsible for this publication of *Max in America* as a classroom textbook.

We at Pro Lingua Associates would like to acknowledge and thank The Experiment Press and its director, Tim McMains, for permission to use the original illustrations and adapt the original text for use in the classroom.

Obviously, this 1987 version of "Max" would not have been possible without the work of all the people who designed and wrote the original material. I was fortunate to have been involved in the original production of the self-study programs as one of the writers of the English program and as Project Director during the final stages of the project.

The key Experiment staff members who initiated the **Poly Training Tape** project with Deutsche Grammophon Gesellschaft were **Georg F. Steinmeyer** and **Alvino E. Fantini**. Those who were responsible for the creation of the basic format, the original characters, and the story line were Alvino, who directed the project for over a year during the first two stages and also wrote the Spanish program with his wife, **Beatriz Fantini**, the writers of the English program, **David Rein**, **Priscilla Martin** and myself, and **Oscar Mesa**, whose wonderful illustrations brought the character and spirit of Max to life.

This edition of "Max" borrows heavily from the original work, but it has also been rewritten and changed considerably. The changes from the original text are my responsibility. I have written some new text and devised a format for using the material in the classroom. I have also provided the procedural directions in the teachers' handbook.

There is, however, still much in the present edition that reflects the thinking and words of the original team. As in any adaptation, it would be pointless to cite what is original and what is revised or new. All that can be said is that, just as the original material was a team effort, this version still reflects the effort of the original team and so I cannot consider myself to be the sole author of this work. We, the original team, are still the authors. The responsibility for this adaptation is, however, mine, and so, Alvino, Bea, David, Priscilla and Oscar, I hope my adaptation meets with your approval.

Raymond C. Clark
February, 1987

Communicating in the Culture:
Max in America

Student's Book Number 1
Student's Book Number 2
Teacher's Handbook
Narrative Picture Posters

Contents

Introduction
to the Student

This book is about Max, a visitor to the United States, and about the Gray family, friends he meets in America. Using *Max in America* in class with your friends and your teacher, you will learn to communicate in English and, while Max learns about the United States, you will too.

We hope you will find *Max* funny and that you will enjoy working with it. Learning English is hard work, but if you have fun and are creative with English, you will quickly learn to speak it. The pictures in this book tell Max's story. You and your friends tell the story in words. When you need help, you should work together to solve your problem, and then if you need to, ask your teacher for suggestions. After you "write the book," you will find model texts at the back of it. Compare your story with the models, but remember that this is your story of Max. If your story does not match the models, that is OK. There are many ways to say the same thing in English.

Using this book, you will practice the English you already know (no matter how much you know) and you will learn lots of vocabulary. You will also learn how to communicate in many different real situations. These situations are listed on the contents page.

People learn languages in many ways, but the most natural way — and we feel the most efficient way — is to play with the language, using your imagination. So, enjoy learning about Max and his American friends. Have fun and be creative!

Introduction to the Teacher

Max in America, Book 2, is the second of two student texts. It is for ESL students at the low intermediate proficiency level. Each of the two texts is made up of 18 units, designed to help the student function in a wide variety of communicative situations, and 12 supplementary narratives.

These student texts contain a minimum of print. They are a sequenced collection of captionless pictures which are open to some interpretation, but they are specific enough to suggest clearly what is going on — a kind of silent movie. You, as both teacher and resource person, should encourage the students working as a team to use their collective English and imaginations to write the captions and to tell Max's story in their own words. If possible, you should encourage them to write in their books. Although initially difficult for students from some cultures, this act will come to symbolize their personal active participation in the creative interplay between the class, the materials, and you. And more importantly, their contributions to *Max*, written into the book, graphically represent their investment in and responsibility for their own learning.

The basic technique for using the book is as follows: The students working together study and discuss the pictures and create conversations and/or narratives that fit the pictures. You, the teacher, then check their work for accuracy and appropriateness. Once the text has been written and approved, the class carries out additional activities that practice and expand on the basic text.

The two student texts are designed to be used with *Max in America, Teacher's Handbook.* It provides detailed, step-by-step descriptions of the procedures to be followed for each unit. These explicit procedural descriptions are intended to be only suggestions, however. Once you have worked through several lessons, closely following the given procedures, you will begin to develop your own variations and will use the material in ways that fit your own personal teaching style and the realities of your teaching situation. The material is open and flexible and you should take advantage of this.

For a fuller explanation of the pedagogical design behind this simple student text, we recommend that you read *Max in America, Teacher's Handbook.*

*The tenses used in the dialogues are indicated
by the shape of the balloons.*

x

Introductory Unit

Unit 1 ◆ Making a Visit

3

1.2

1.3

1.4

1.5

1.6

1.7

1.8

1.9

1.10

1.11

1.12

1.13

7

1.14

2.1

Unit 2 ♦ Talking about Birthdays

2.2

2.3

2.4

2.5

2.6

2.7

Bill   Betty   Anne   John

2.8

2.9

3.1

Unit 3 ◆ Talking about Traveling

3.2

3.3

3.4

3.5

3.6

3.7

15

3.8

3.9

3.10

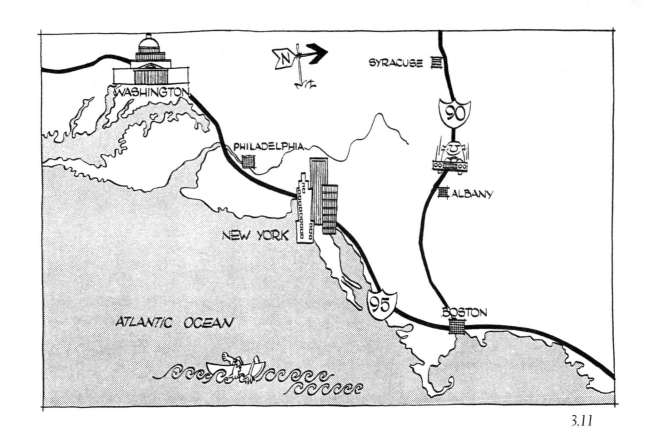

3.11

4.1

Unit 4 ◆ Looking for Something

4.2

4.3

4.4

4.5

4.6

4.7

4.8

4.9

4.10

4.11

4.12

4.13

4.14

4.15

PARK
HOTEL

Sunday, July 19th

Dear Mr and Mrs Gray,

Thank you very much for inviting me to your house last night. It was wonderful to see all of you again, and I was pleased to meet Ted. You are a very friendly family; you make me feel at home.

I'll be sure to send you some post cards while I'm on my trip. I look forward to seeing you again when I come back to New York.

Sincerely yours,
Max

5.1

Going to a Party ◆ Unit 5

5.3

5.2

29

5.4

5.5

5.6

30

5.7

31

5.8

6.1

Unit 6 ◆ Saying Goodnight and Making Plans   33

6.2

6.3

6.4

6.5

6.6

6.7

6.8

6.9

7.1

Unit 7 ◆ Going on a Business Trip

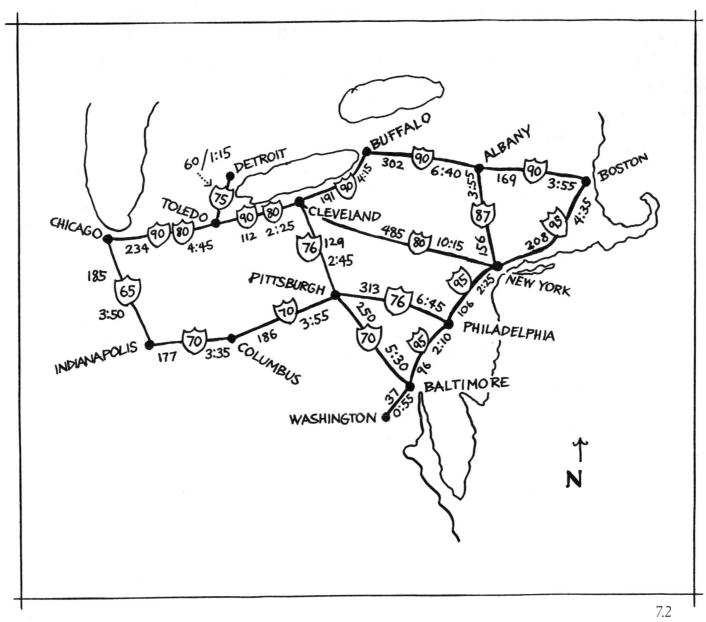

7.3

7.4

7.6

7.5

8.1

Buying Groceries ◆ Unit 8

8.2

8.3

43

Groceries

Bakery

Dairy

Beverages

Produce

Meat

Fish

Poultry

Other

8.4

8.5

9.1

9.2

9.3

9.4

Unit 9 ◆ Talking about the Weather

45

9.5

9.6

9.7

9.8

48

9.10

9.9

Centigrade and Fahrenheit

−20° C. = −4° F.		15° C. = 59° F.
−15° C. = 5° F.		20° C. = 68° F.
−10° C. = 14° F.		25° C. = 77° F.
− 5° C. = 23° F.		30° C. = 86° F.
0° C. = 32° F. (freezing)		35° C. = 95° F.
5° C. = 41° F.		100° C. = 212° F. (boiling)
10° C. = 50° F.		

9.11

$$C° = \frac{5}{9}(F° - 32)$$
$$F° = \frac{9}{5}C° + 32$$

50

9.12

51

9.13

10.1

10.2

10.3

Unit 10 ◆ Weddings and Births

10.4

10.5

10.7

10.6

55

10.9

10.8

10.10

10.11

10.12

Later —

10.13

10.15

10.14

10.16

10.17

60

11.1

Unit 11 ◆ Being Interviewed

APPLICATION FOR EMPLOYMENT

INSTRUCTIONS: Fill out this application completely. Do not omit any answers. Do not erase. Draw a line through incorrect responses. **Print** your responses in CAPITAL LETTERS (ABCDEF, etc.).

1 Name

_____
(last)   (first)   (middle initial)

_____

2 Home address
Number and Street: _____

City: _____

State or Province: _____

Country: _____

8 Check the appropriate square:

RELIGION	EDUATION	MARITAL STATUS
☐ Catholic	☐ Primary	☐ Single
☐ Protestant	☐ Secondary	☐ Married
☐ Jewish	☐ University (B.A.)	☐ Divorced
☐ Moslem	☐ M.A.	☐ Separated
☐ Buddhist	☐ Ph.D.	☐ Widowed
☐ other	☐ other	

3 Mailing address (if different from above):

4 Sex
Circle one: 5 Age:

M   F

6 Date of birth

_____
(Month)   (Day)   (Year)

9 References — List the names and addresses of three people who know you well.

a _____
   _____
   _____

b _____
   _____
   _____

c _____
   _____
   _____

7 Cross out the inappropriate words:

I have
I have not applied for employment here before.

10 Signature

11 Today's date

Form 000-×

Check over your answers!

11.3

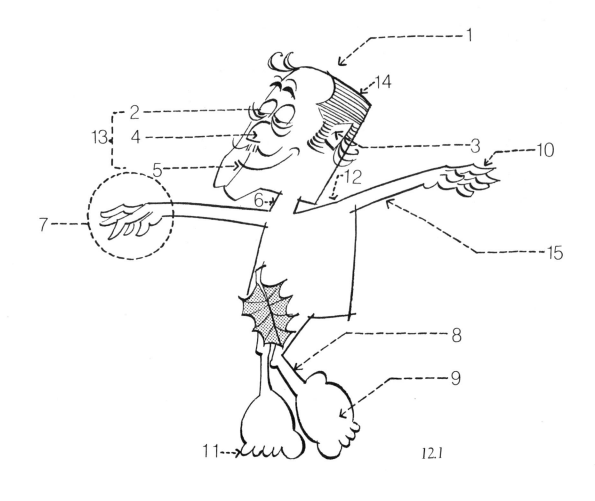

12.1

12.2

12.3

12.4

12.5

12.6

13.1

Unit 13 ◆ Visiting the Doctor

13.2

13.3

13.4

13.5

13.6

13.7

13.8

13.9

13.10

13.11

14.1

Unit 14 ◆ Talking about Traveling

73

14.2

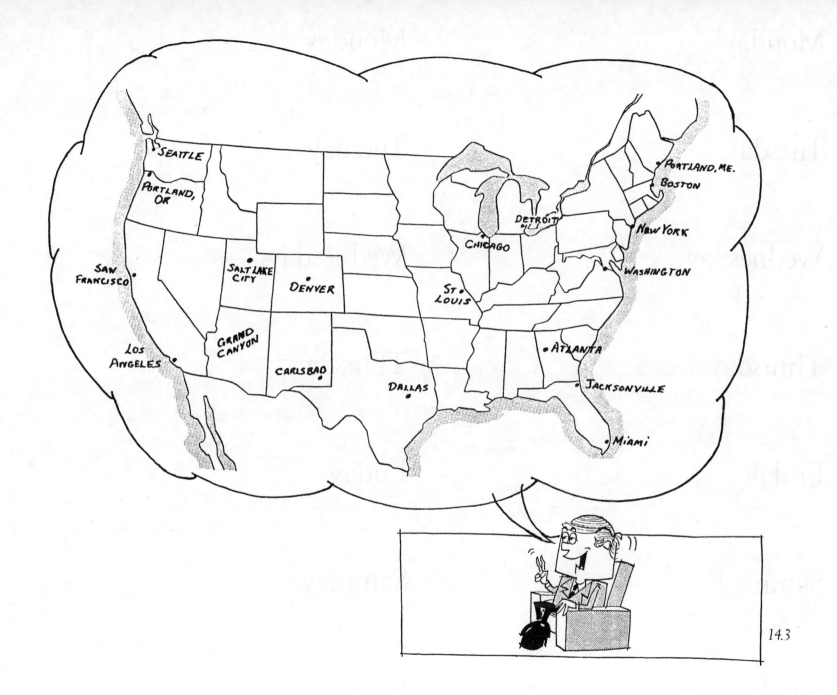

14.3

Monday	Monday
Tuesday	Tuesday
Wednesday	Wednesday
Thursday	Thursday
Friday	Friday
Saturday	Saturday
Sunday	Sunday

14.4

15.1

Playing Sports and Games ◆ Unit 15

15.2

15.3

15.4

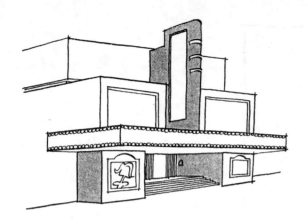

16.1

Going to the Movies ◆ **Unit 16**

16.2

16.3

16.4

17.1

Talking about and
Playing with Language ◆ Unit 17

Language	Country or Region	Number of Speakers (in millions)	People
Chinese (Mandarin, Cantonese, Wu, Min, and Hakka)	China	976	Chinese
English	The United Kingdom, The United States, Canada, Australia, New Zealand	420	English(men), Americans, Canadians, Australians, New Zealanders
Hindi and Urdu	India, Pakistan	382	Indians, Pakistani
Spanish	Spain, Latin America	296	Spaniards, Latin Americans
Russian	The Union of Soviet Socialist Republics	285	Russians (Soviets)
Arabic	The Middle East, North Africa	177	Egyptians, Syrians, Saudis, Moroccans, Lebanese, Libyans, Algerians, Tunisians, Iraqis, Kuwaitis, etc.
Bengali	Bangladesh, India	171	Bengalis, Indians
Portuguese	Portugal, Brazil	164	Portuguese, Brazilians
Malay/Indonesian	Malaysia, Indonesia	128	Malaysians, Indonesians
Japanese	Japan	122	Japanese
German	German, Switzerland, Austria	118	Germans, Swiss, Austrians
French	France, Belgium, Haiti, Switzerland, Canada	114	French(men), Belgians, Haitians, Swiss, Austrians
Punjabi	Pakistan, India	72	Pakistanis, Indians
Korean	Korea	66	Koreans
Italian	Italy	63	Italians

Source of figures: The World Almanac and Book Facts, 1987.

17.3

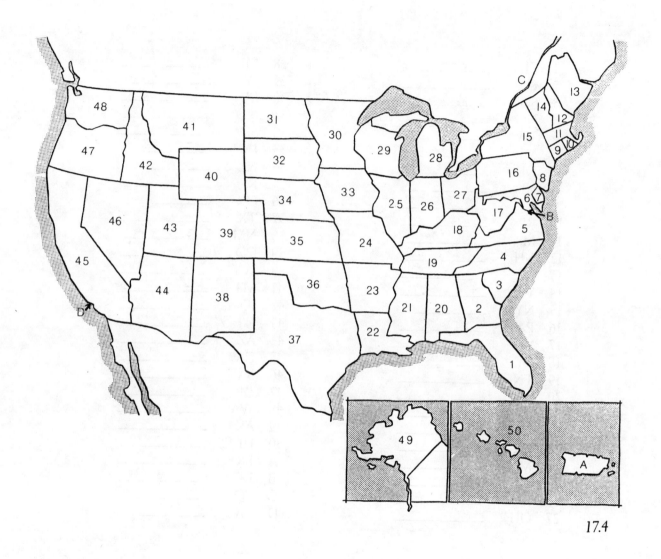

17.4

1	FL	————	28	MI	————
2	GA	————	29	WI	————
3	SC	————	30	MN	————
4	NC	————	31	ND	————
5	VA	————	32	SD	————
6	MD	————	33	IA	————
7	DE	————	34	NE	————
8	NJ	————	35	KS	————
9	CT	————	36	OK	————
10	RI	————	37	TX	————
11	MA	————	38	NM	————
12	NH	————	39	CO	————
13	ME	————	40	WY	————
14	VT	————	41	MT	————
15	NY	————	42	ID	————
16	PA	————	43	UT	————
17	WV	————	44	AZ	————
18	KY	————	45	CA	————
19	TN	————	46	NV	————
20	AL	————	47	OR	————
21	MS	————	48	WA	————
22	LA	————	49	AK	————
23	AR	————	50	HI	————
24	MO	————	A	PR	————
25	IL	————	B	DC	————
26	IN	————	C	PQ	————
27	OH	————	D	LA	————

18.1

Unit 18 ◆ Saying Goodbye

18.2

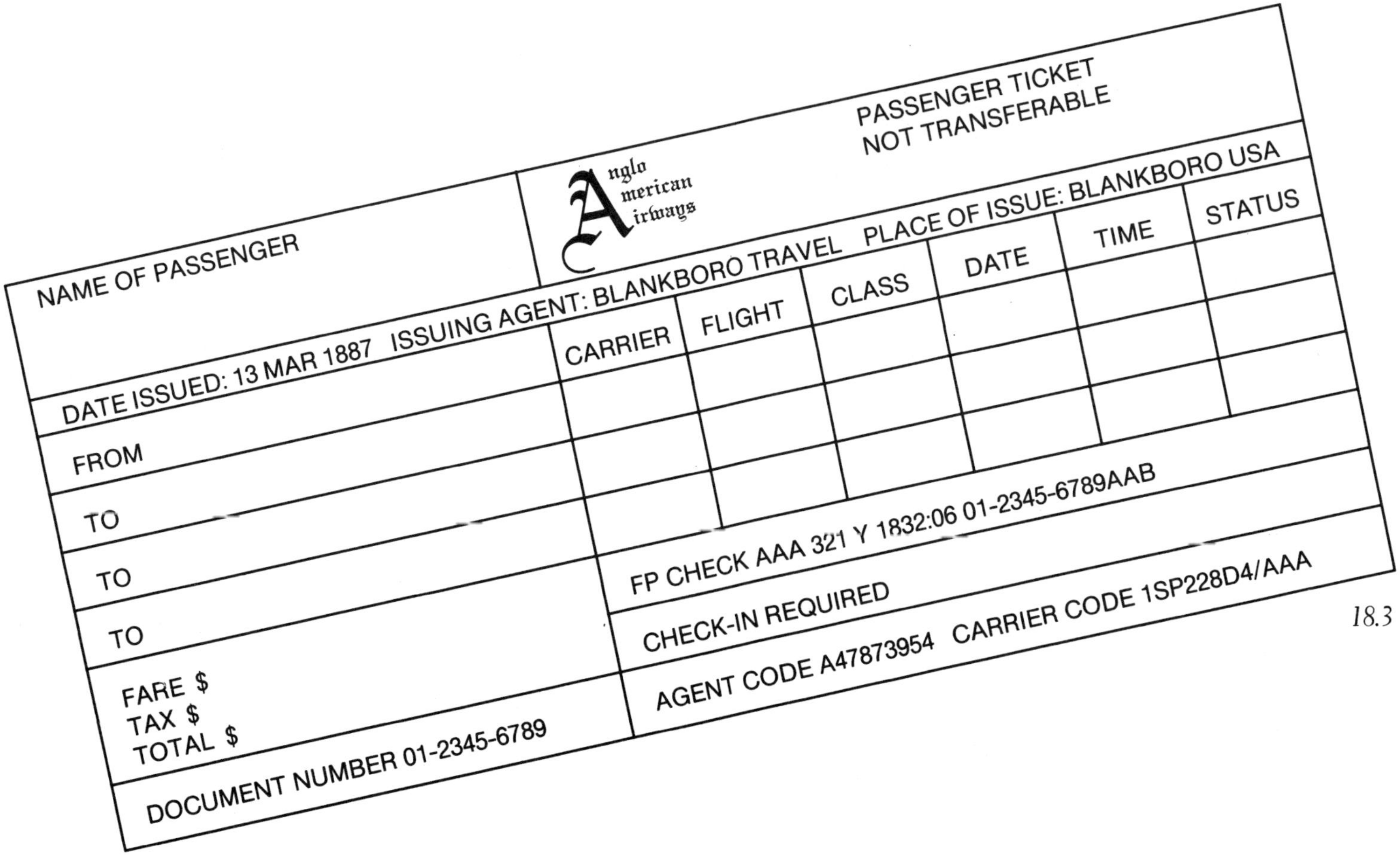

PASSENGER TICKET
NOT TRANSFERABLE

Anglo American Airways

PLACE OF ISSUE: BLANKBORO USA

NAME OF PASSENGER

ISSUING AGENT: BLANKBORO TRAVEL

DATE ISSUED: 13 MAR 1887

CARRIER	FLIGHT	CLASS	DATE	TIME	STATUS

FROM

TO

TO   FP CHECK AAA 321 Y 1832:06 01-2345-6789AAB

TO   CHECK-IN REQUIRED

FARE $ AGENT CODE A47873954   CARRIER CODE 1SP228D4/AAA
TAX $
TOTAL $

DOCUMENT NUMBER 01-2345-6789

CARRIER CODE 1SP228D4/AAA

18.3

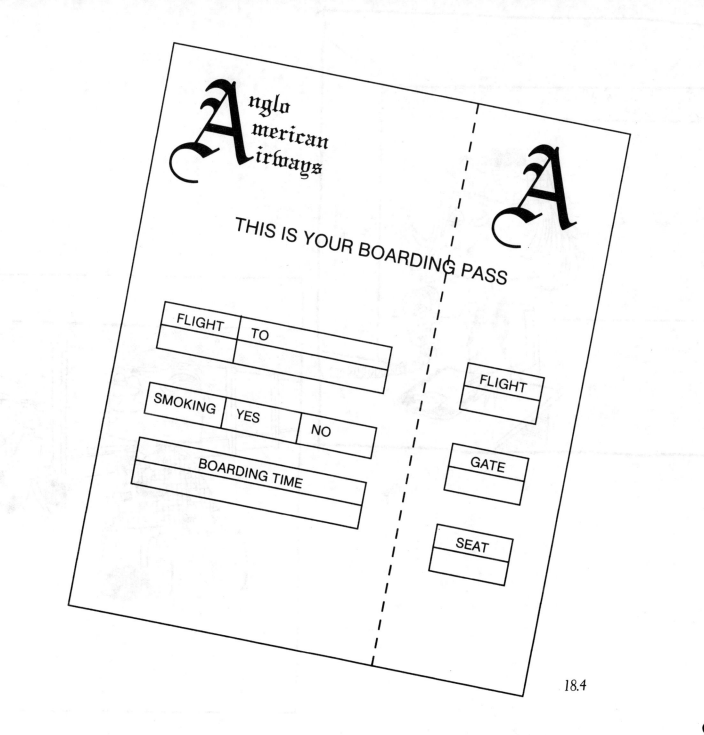

18.4

18.5

Narrative
Pictures

bus station
unfortunately
baggage
driver
loss

roadside
missed
hitchhiking
pick . . . up
confused
according to

rent
choice
sedan
convertible
economy car
choose

N16

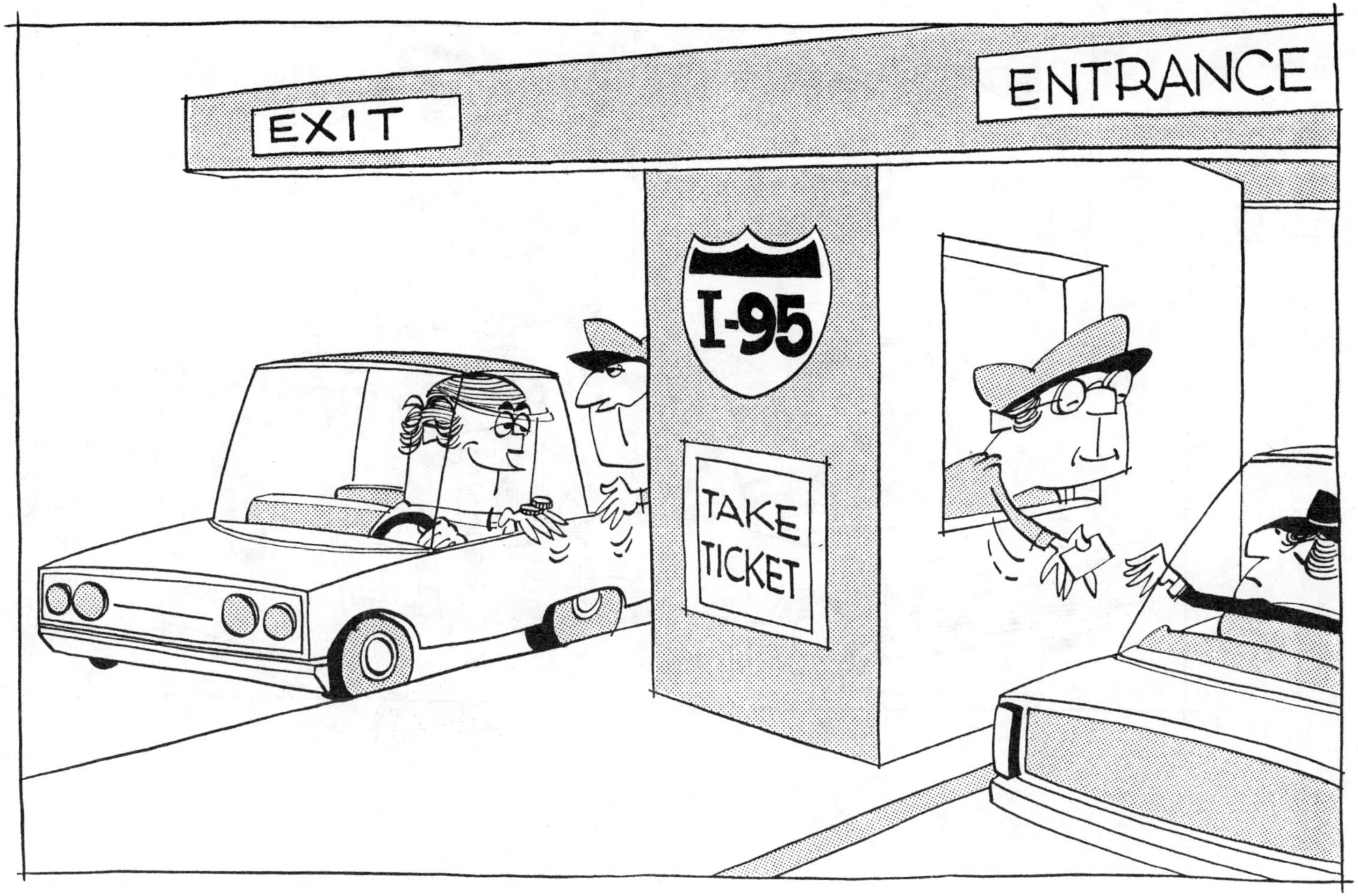
EXIT
ENTRANCE
I-95
TAKE TICKET

interchange
toll
toll booth
attendant
collecting
giving out

service station
fill up
check
oil
charge
credit card

stopped
speeding
informs
speed limit
worried
fine

N19

accident
run into
furious
license
traffic light

country
relatives
farm
showing around
farmyard
cousins

park
bench
couple
feeding
admiring
as usual

argument
listen to
folk
classical
rock
calm down

getting ready
church
ironing
pressing
iron
wrinkled

gather
exchange
gifts
unwrapped
presents
toy

The Texts

Book 2: Introductory Unit

A.   *This is Max. He's from _____*. Max is a tourist, visiting the United States. On the plane to New York, he met Mr. and Mrs. Gray and their daughter, Kathy. The Grays invited him to visit them at their home. Max has been sightseeing in New York City. He has been staying at the Park Hotel.*

After Max Visits the Grays, he's going to take a trip around the United States.

B.   *This is the Gray family. Mr. and Mrs. Gray and Kathy met Max on the plane. Their young son, Ted, was not on the plane with them. They have invited Max to visit them. Max is going to meet Ted for the first time.*

Unit 1: Making a Visit

1.1   1 *steps*   *Mr. Gray has picked Max up at the Park Hotel*
        2 *garage*   *and brought him to the Gray's house.*
        3 *driveway*

1.2   *Mrs. Gray: Hello, Max.*

1.3   *Mrs. Gray: It's so nice to see you again.*

1.4   *Max: Hello, Mrs. Gray. It's good to be here . . .*

1.5   *Max: . . . and I'm glad to see you, Kathy.*

1.6   *Kathy: Hi, Max.*

1.7   *Kathy: I'd like you to meet my little brother, Ted.*

1.8   *Kathy: Ted, this is Max.*

1.9   *Max: Hello, Ted. I'm happy to meet you.*

1.10   *Ted: Hi, Max. What's that in your hand?*

1.11   *Max: This is some candy for the family.*

1.12   *Mrs. Gray: Why, thank you, Max. That's very thoughtful of you.*
        Max: Not at all.

1.13   *Ted: Mom, can I have a piece of candy now?*
        Mrs. Gray: Later, dear.

1.14   *Kathy is talking with her friend Betty. Betty asked Kathy who her new friend was. Kathy said that his name was Max. Betty asked where she had met him. Kathy explained that she had met him on a plane when she and her parents were returning to New York. Betty asked where he was from. Kathy told her that he was from _____ . Betty commented that he was very cute.*

Unit 2: Talking about Birthdays

2.1   *The bookcase is against the wall. There are two cabinets under the bookcase. A lamp hangs from the ceiling. There is a rug on the floor. The Grays and Max are walking across the room.*

2.2   *Max: How old are you, Ted?*
        Ted: I'm ten, almost eleven.

2.3   *Max: When will you be eleven?*
        Ted: Next month. My birthday is coming soon. It's on November 13th.

2.4   *Ted: How old are you, Max?*

2.5 *Kathy: Ted! That's not polite. Don't know better?*
Ted: Well, he asked me. Can't I ask him?

2.6 *Max: That's O.K. I don't mind. I'm 23.*

2.7 *Ted: You're older than my sister. She's 19.*

2.8 *Bill: 22 ,   February 13, 19 ____*
Betty: 20 ,   October 30, 19 ____
Anne: 21 ,   August 21, 19 ____
John: 23 ,   July 16, 19 ____

2.9 *It's Ted's eleventh birthday. There are eleven candles on the cake. Ted*

Unit 3: Talking about Traveling

3.1 *flowers   Mr. and Mrs. Gray are about to sit down on the*
a vase   sofa. Max is about to tell them about his week in
a sofa   New York.
an ashtray
an armchair

3.2 *Mr. Gray: Where did you go last week, Max?*
Max: Well, for one thing I went shopping.

3.3 *Mr. Gray: Where else did you go?*

3.4 *Max: I had dinner in two restaurants, one good one and one bad one.*

3.5 *Mr. Gray: Did you go to any museums?*

3.6 *Max: I went to two different art museums.*

3.7 *Mr. Gray: What are you going to do next?*

3.8 *Max: Well, I want to see more of the countryside . . .*

3.9 *Max: . . . so I'm going to take a trip around the U.S.*

3.10 *Bill: So, John, tell me about your trip from Syracuse*
–3.11 *to Richmond.*

Unit 4: Looking for Something

4.1 *Max is putting on his coat. He's about to leave. The Grays are about to say goodbye to him because he's leaving.*

4.2 *Uh-oh.*

4.3 *Max: I can't find my key. It was in my pocket, but I don't think I have it now.*

4.4 *Kathy: It's probably in the closet.*

4.5 *Kathy: No, it's not on the closet floor.*
Ted: Maybe it's under the sofa.

4.6 *Ted: I'll look there.*

4.7 *Ted: No, I can't find it.*

4.8 *Kathy: Here it is on the living room rug.*

4.9 *Max: Oh, thanks, Kathy.*

4.10 *Max: Now I guess I'm ready to leave.*
Mr. Gray: I'll drive you back to the hotel, Max.

4.11 *Max: That's very kind of you, Mr. Gray.*

4.12 *Max: Good night, everyone.*
All: Good night, Max.

4.13 *Kathy: Come back again soon.*

4.14 *Anne: Where did you ever <u>find</u> that beautiful sweater?*
Betty: I <u>found</u> it at the thrift shop.

111

Anne: Really? I've never <u>come across</u> much there that I liked.

Betty: Well, you have to <u>look around</u> a little. Just yesterday I <u>discovered</u> a beautiful leather jacket for only $20.

Anne: I <u>find</u> that hard to believe. I was there just two days ago, and I <u>looked over</u> **all** the clothes. I didn't see any leather jackets.

Betty: Well, you must have <u>overlooked</u> it.

Anne: I've been <u>searching</u> everywhere for an inexpensive leather jacket. Is the thrift shop open now?

Betty: I'm not sure.

Anne: How can we <u>find out</u>?

Betty: Let's <u>look up</u> their ad in the yellow pages.

Anne: Uh . . . Sorry, I've <u>misplaced</u> the phone book.

Betty: You've <u>lost</u> the phone book?

Anne: Well, at least I <u>can't find</u> it. Yesterday I <u>hunted</u> everywhere for it.

Betty: Where can it be?

Anne: The last time I saw it, it was in its usual place, right beside the phone.

Betty: You're always <u>losing</u> things. I'd <u>lose</u> my mind if I had to live with you.

Anne: Now, don't <u>lose</u> your temper. I'm sure that if we <u>look for</u> it, we'll <u>find</u> it.

Betty: Ah! I see it.

Anne: Where?

Betty: <u>Look</u> over there — on top of the refrigerator.

Anne: Oh, yeah.

Betty: Now, let's <u>look up</u> the listing for the thrift shop. Here it is: 375 Commerce, and they're open. Want to drive over?

Anne: We can't.

Betty: Why not?

Anne: The car keys are <u>missing</u>.

Betty: What? Anne, you are a <u>loser!</u>

Unit 5: Going to a Party

5.1   Max and Kathy are at a party. They're having a drink. The couple on the left is chatting, and the couple on the right is dancing to music from a record player.

5.2   Max: Can I get you another drink?
Kathy: No thanks. I think I've had enough.

5.3   Max: Who is that woman over there?
Kathy: You mean the tall, thin blonde?

5.4   Max: No, the brunette behind her.
Kathy: Oh, her. I don't know what her name is . . .

5.5   Kathy: . . . Why do you ask?

5.6   Max: Because her dress is just like yours.

5.8   Bill/Betty: How was the party last night?
John/Anne:

Unit 6: Saying Goodnight and Making Plans

6.1   Max is bringing Kathy home in a taxi. They were at a party. They will go to the door and say good night. The cabbie will wait for Max and take him back to the Park Hotel.

6.2   Max: That party was fun.
Kathy: I'm glad you enjoyed it.

6.3   Kathy: I'm sorry you're leaving New York tomorrow.

6.4 *Max: So am I, but I want to see the rest of the country.*

6.5 *Kathy: Will we see you again before you go home?*
Max: Well, I'll be in New York for several days at the end of my trip.

6.6 *Kathy: Will you call then?*
Max: I certainly will. I want to see you again.

6.7 *Ted: Hey Max, aren't you going to kiss her good night?*

6.8
1 *an ocean/a sea*
2 *a plateau*
3 *a forest*
4 *some hills*
5 *some mountains*
6 *a lake*
7 *a river*
8 *a bay*
9 *an island*
10 *a plain*
11 *a dam*
12 *a reservoir*
13 *a pond*
14 *a swamp*
15 *a volcano*
16 *a waterfall*
17 *a beach*
18 *a delta*

Unit 7: Going on a Business Trip

7.1   *It's Monday morning. Mr. Gray will be away this week. He's going on a business trip. He's going to take his own car and drive to _____ . He'll be back again on Friday. Now he's backing the car out of the driveway as the family waves goodbye.*

7.3
1 *headlight*
2 *license plate*
3 *bumper*
4 *tire*
5 *wheel*
6 *trunk*
7 *steering wheel*
8 *windshield*
9 *windshield wiper*
10 *roof*
11 *tail light*
12 *hood*
13 *engine (under hood)*

7.4 *The car is out of gas; the gas tank is empty. Ralph'll have to get some gas.*

7.5 *The car has a flat tire. Ralph will have to change the tire.*

7.6 *There was an accident. The car hit a tree. Ralph is injured. He'll have to go to the hospital.*

Unit 8: Buying Groceries

8.1 *Grocer: Anything else, Mrs. Gray?*
–8.2 *Mrs. Gray: I was going to get a box of Presto detergent. Don't you have any?*
Grocer: I'm afraid it's all gone. But we're supposed to get some more tomorrow.
Mrs. Gray: Oh dear. I'm all out of detergent, and I've got to do the laundry today.
Grocer: Try Super. It's supposed to be very good.
Mrs. Gray: Well, I've got to get something, so I might as well get Super.

8.3
three bottles of soda
a box of detergent
two cans of sardines
two 2-pound bags of sugar
two packages of spaghetti
two jars of olives

8.4
bakery products
dairy products
beverages
produce
meat
fish
poultry

Unit 9: Talking about the Weather

9.1-4   *In the spring the weather becomes mild. Temperatures are warm. Everything turns green. In summer the sun is often hot. In fall the weather turns cool. The leaves fall from the trees. Sometimes it is windy. In winter it is cold. In the North it snows.*

113

9.5 Mr. Gray: Would you turn on the radio, dear? It's time for the weather report.
Mrs. Gray: Just a minute.

9.6 (Mrs. Gray turns on the radio.)

9.7 Announcer: The present temperature is 50 degrees. It will be cloudy today, with a 70% chance of rain.

9.8 Mrs. Gray: Oh dear! Rain again. I must remember to take my umbrella.

9.9 Announcer: It will be sunny and warmer tomorrow, with a high of 60.

9.10 Mr. Gray: Well, at least tomorrow will be nice.

9.12 1. It's warm. He's wearing light clothing.
2. It's hot. He's wearing shorts and sandals.
3. It's cool. He's wearing a sweater.
4. It's cold. He's wearing a coat, a scarf, a hat, and boots.
5. It's freezing. He's wearing an overcoat.
6. It's snowing.
7. It's raining. He's wearing a raincoat and carrying an umbrella.
8. It's windy.
9. It's foggy.

Unit 10: Weddings and Births

10.1 couple   boyfriend
in love   girlfriend

10.2 engaged
engagement ring

10.3 wedding   groom
bride   wedding rings

10.4 reception
toast

10.5 anniversary

10.6 The door bell rings.

10.7 Mrs. Gray: I heard that the Cranes' daughter got married.
Mrs. Stewart: Yes, and it was a big wedding.

10.8 Mrs. Gray: How many bridesmaids did she have?
Mrs. Stewart: Oh, about ten.

10.9 Mrs. Grey: Did they have a reception?
Mrs. Stewart: Yes, at the country club.

10.10 Mrs. Stewart: They had a band and 300 guests.

10.11 Mrs. Gray: That must have cost a lot of money.
Mrs. Stewart: Oh yes, but Mr. Crane has a lot of money.

10.12 Mrs. Stewart: Ellen, have you heard the news?
Mrs. Gray: Did your daughter have her baby?

10.13 Mrs. Stewart: Yes she did. At 8:39 last night.

10.14 Mrs. Gray: Congratulations! Was it a boy or a girl?
Mrs. Stewart: A baby boy.

10.15 Mrs. Stewart: And he weighs 10 pounds, 2 ounces.
Mrs. Gray: What a big baby!

10.16 Mrs. Stewart: And he is 22 inches long.

10.17 Mrs. Gray: He'll probably be big like his father.
Mrs. Stewart: Yes, my son-in-law is 6'4" tall.

The Texts ◆ Book 2

Unit 11: Being Interviewed

11.1   *Kathy is looking for a job. She has applied for a position as a reporter. She has filled out an application, and she has given it to the man at the desk — the interviewer. Kathy is the applicant. Now she's having an interview. The interviewer has asked her some questions. Now he's listening to Kathy's response.*

Unit 12: Talking about Health and Condition

12.1
1 head	7 hand	12 shoulder
2 eye	8 leg	13 face
3 ear	9 foot	14 hair
4 nose	10 finger	15 arm
5 mouth, lips	11 toe	
6 neck		

12.2   Mr. Gray: *Hello, Henry. How are you today?*
Mr. Stewart: *I'm not feeling very well, David.*

12.3   Mr. Gray: *Why? What's the matter?*
Mr. Stewart: *I have a bad pain in my leg. I think it's arthritis.*

12.4   Mr. Gray: *I'm sorry to hear that. Are you going to see a doctor?*

12.5   Mr. Stewart: *I went to the doctor last week. He told me to take some aspirin.*

12.6   Mr. Gray: *Are you feeling better than you were?*
Mr. Stewart: *No, I'm not. My leg still hurts, so I'm going back to see the doctor again.*

Unit 13: Visiting the Doctor

13.1   1 cast
2 crutch
3 nurse/receptionist
4 cane

Mr. Stewart is at the doctor's office. He's in the waiting room. He and the other man are the doctor's patients.

13.2   Nurse: *Mr. Stewart, the doctor will see you now.*

13.3   Mr. Stewart: *Doctor, my leg still hurts, and the aspirin doesn't help.*

13.4   Doctor: *Well, do you have any other problems?*

13.5   Mr. Stewart: *No. I sleep all right. My appetite is good. I never have headaches.*

13.6   Mr. Stewart: *It's just that my leg still aches.*

13.7   *The doctor examines Mr. Stewart's leg.*

13.8   Doctor: *Here. I'll give you a prescription for something stronger than aspirin.*

3.9   Mr. Stewart: *Thank you, doctor.*
Doctor: *If there's no improvement in a few days, call me.*

13.10
aspirin	cough syrup
bandage	eye drops
pills	antihistamine
ointment	antacid

13.11   Anne: *Hello.*

John: *Hi, Anne. How are you today?*

Anne: *How do you think I am? (cough, cough)*

John: *You have a bad cough, don't you?*

Anne: *Achoo!*

John: *And you're sneezing. Did you take any aspirin?*

Anne: *Yes, I took some aspirin and some other medicine. I even drank some whiskey. But my head still and my eyes sting,*

115

my nose is stuffed up, and my ears ache, and I have a sore throat. I feel miserable.

John: Sounds like you've got either a bad cold or the flu. How did you get it?

Anne: Oh, I don't know. I think I got it from you. Or maybe from Steve, or from Pete, or Jack or Don or . . .

Unit 14: Talking about Traveling

14.1   *Max has returned from his trip around the United States. The Grays have come to the bus station to pick him up. He'll stay with the Grays for a few days before he goes home.*

Unit 15: Playing Sports and Games

15.1   *It's Saturday afternoon. Mr. Gray doesn't work on Saturday. He goes to the golf course with a friend. Today he's playing golf with Mr. Todd. Mr. Gray doesn't play golf very well and neither does Mr. Todd, but they both like to play.*

15.2   *On Saturday afternoon Mrs. Gray goes over to Mrs. Stewart's house. She plays cards with her neighbors. She plays quite well and her neighbors do, too. They all enjoy playing cards.*

15.3   *On Saturday afternoon Kathy doesn't attend classes. She usually goes to the tennis courts with her friends. Today Kathy is playing with Max. Kathy doesn't play tennis very well, and Max doesn't either. But they both enjoy tennis.*

15.4   *Ted doesn't go to school on Saturday. He plays with his playmates. Today they're playing marbles in the Grays' back yard. Ted plays marbles very well, and so do his playmates. They don't like to go to school, but they really enjoy playing marbles.*

Unit 16: Going to the Movies

16.1   *It's Saturday evening. Mr. Gray played golf almost all afternoon. Now he would like to see a movie. He would like to see a mystery. Mr. Gray also likes westerns, but he would rather see a mystery this evening.*

16.2   *Mrs. Gray played cards all afternoon. She would like to see a musical. Mrs. Gray also likes love stories, but this evening she would rather see the musical.*

16.3   *Kathy played tennis with Max for two hours this afternoon. Now she would like to see a movie. She likes love stories and musicals, but tonight she would prefer to see a love story.*

16.4   *Ted played with his playmates all day long. Now he would like to see a western. He also likes mysteries, but he would rather see a western.*

Unit 17: Talking about and Playing with Language

17.1   *The Grays are looking at a globe with Max. They're talking about languages. Mr. Gray says, "Portuguese is spoken in Portugal and Brazil by about ———— million Portuguese and Brazilians."*

17.2   *Max and the Grays are playing a word game. Max says, "I've got an A, two E's, two I's, an O, and a U. What can I spell with that?" Kathy says, "You've got only vowels. You need some consonants." Ted says, "I'll trade you two consonants for two vowels." Max asks, "Which ones?" Ted says, "An X and an H."*

Unit 18: Saying Goodbye

18.1   Your attention, please! This is the first call for flight 273 to _____ . All passengers, please report to Gate 22A for boarding.

18.2   It's time to say goodbye. Max is leaving New York. In a few hours he will be arriving in _____ . Tomorrow at this time Kathy be thinking of Max, and Max will be thinking of Kathy. They will miss each other. A week from now they will be writing each other letters. If Kathy gets a job as a reporter and earns enough money, she might be visiting Max in _____ a year from now.

18.5   Your attention, please. This is the final call for _____ (airlines) flight _____ to _____ . All ticket holders, please report to gate _____ for boarding.

Book 2: Narrative Pictures

N13   bus station
unfortunately
baggage
driver
loss

Max is at a bus station. Unfortunately, he has lost his baggage. The bus driver tells him to report his loss at the lost and found window.

N14   roadside
missed
hitchhiking
pick . . . up
confused
according to

Max is standing on the roadside. He has missed his bus. Now he is hitchhiking, but nobody will pick him up. Max is confused. According to the sign, New York is in the other direction.

N15   rent
choice
sedan
convertible
economy car
choose

Max is going to rent a car. He has a choice of three models: a sedan, a convertible, or an economy car. The saleswoman asks Max to choose one of the cars.

N16   interchange
toll
toll booth
attendant
collecting
giving out

Max is at an interchange on a highway. He is paying the toll at a toll booth. One attendant is collecting the toll while the other one is giving out tickets to cars that enter the highway.

N17   service station
fill up
check
oil
charge
credit card

Max is at a service station. He asks the attendant to fill it up with gas. The attendant asks if Max wants him to check the oil and water. Max asks if he can charge his purchase with a credit card.

N18   stopped
speeding
informs
speed limit
worried
fine

Max has been stopped for speeding. The police officer informs him that the speed limit is 55. Max is worried because he may have to pay a fine.

N19   accident
run into
furious
license
traffic light

Max has had an accident. He has run into another car. The driver of the other car is furious. Max is showing his license to the police officer and explaining that he didn't see a traffic light.

N20   country
relatives
farm
showing around
farmyard
cousins

The Grays are in the country. They are visiting some relatives who live on a farm. Their relatives are showing them around the farmyard. Ted and Kathy are talking to their cousins.

N21 *park*
bench
couple
feeding
admiring
as usual

The Grays are in a park. Mr. and Mrs. Gray are sitting on a bench. Mrs. Gray is looking at the couple on the next bench. Ted is feeding the pigeons. Kathy is admiring the fountain. Mr. Gray is reading the paper as usual.

N22 *argument*
listen to
folk
classical
rock
calm down

The Grays are having an argument. Kathy wants to listen to folk music, Mr. Gray wants to listen to classical music, and Ted wants to listen to rock. Mrs. Gray is trying to calm them down.

N23 *getting ready*
church
ironing
pressing
iron
wrinkled

It's Sunday morning. The Grays are getting ready to go to church. Mrs. Gray is doing some ironing. She's pressing a pair of pants with an iron. Kathy is waiting to use the iron because her dress is wrinkled.

N24 *gather*
exchange
gifts
unwrapped
presents
toy

It's Christmas. On Christmas morning the Grays gather around the Christmas tree to exchange gifts. Ted has unwrapped one of his presents. It's a toy truck.